Editor
Tracy Edmunds

Editorial Project Manager
Mara Ellen Guckian

Illustrators
Alexandra Artigas
Esmerelda Stevens
Kevin McCarthy

Cover Artist
Denise Bauer

Managing Editor
Ina Massler Levin, M.A.

Creative Director
Karen J. Goldfluss, M.S. Ed.

Art Production Manager
Kevin Barnes

Art Coordinator
Renée Christine Yates

Imaging
Rosa C. See

Publisher
Mary D. Smith, M.S. Ed.

Standard-Based

Full-Color

Science Games

Grades Pre•K–K

- Inquiry-based Activities
- Explorations
- Graphs

Life Science

Physical Science

Earth Science

P9-CAL-478

Authors

Bridget Kilroy Hoffman
Julie Mauer, M.A.

Teacher Created Resources, Inc.
6421 Industry Way
Westminster, CA 92683
www.teachercreated.com
ISBN: 978-1-4206-8334-9
©2007 Teacher Created Resources, Inc.
Reprinted, 2009
Made in U.S.A.

Teacher Created Resources

Table of Contents

Introduction

Science Games is a collection of hands-on explorations, brightly illustrated board games, and great graphing activities that offer young learners opportunities for "doing" science. The activities in this book will stimulate and assist students to actively construct and develop their own understandings of science. *Science Games* is designed for the creative kindergarten teacher who strives to provide his or her students with an inquiry approach to "doing" science. Science in the early years should be focused on students asking questions, doing investigations, manipulating tools to gather data, making observations, and communicating explanations. *Science Games* provides teachers with quick and easy hands-on explorations that spark curiosity and ignite a high interest in various science concepts appropriate for young learners. After "doing" a science exploration, students will be confident and excited to practice and apply their new knowledge using the corresponding games and graphing activities.

Student inquiry has an essential role in the process of "doing" science in the various disciplines of physical science, life science, and Earth and space science. Use the games and activities in this book to provide students with a playful way to demonstrate their science knowledge and to nurture children's constant curiosity about the world around them. This valuable teacher resource is organized by the three science disciplines with emphasis on inquiry in each. The concepts covered are important components of the science disciplines appropriate for young children and are aligned with national science content standards and many state early learning guidelines.

Inquiry

- Ask questions about the environment
- Plan and conduct a simple investigation
- Use simple tools to gather data
- Construct explanations
- Communicate investigations and explanations

Physical Science

- Properties of objects and materials
- Position and motion of objects

Earth and Space Science

- Changes in earth and sky

Life Science

- The characteristics of organisms
- Organisms and environments

Teaching Tools

Science Games includes four fabulous tools for teaching each concept:

- **Tidbits for Teachers** are simple facts and concise general science knowledge to prepare teachers for each lesson.
- **Energizing Explorations** provide hands-on investigations for introducing and exploring the science concepts. This icon 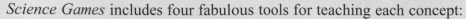 indicates the introductory exploration for each unit.
- **Full-Color Games** provide fun ways to apply and practice their new science knowledge.
- **Great Graphs** give students the opportunity to graph their knowledge in a variety of ways to demonstrate science learning.

Helpful Hints for Using the Games

The colorful, attractive games in this book are easy and time efficient to make. Just follow the simple directions outlined in the *Preparation* section of each *Directions* page to create great games that can be used in the classroom in a matter of minutes. There are multiple options for using these cooperative games in the classroom.

- **Small Group**—Have two, three, or four students play together or with the teacher.
- **Partners**—Allow two students to play together.
- **Center Activities**—Place the games in a science center to reinforce whole-group instruction.
- **Individual Assessment**—Have one student complete a game independently, then check the game to assess student progress.
- **Family Fun**—Send the game home with students for further enhancement of science skills. See pages 173–174 for the family letter and directions.

Note: It is important to review each set of picture cards with students before playing a game. Some pictures could be interpreted in more than one way.

Game Assembly and Storage

The games are easy to assemble. Below are suggestions on how to prepare and store them.

- Using a color photocopy machine, copy the games and keep the original book as your master, OR dismantle the entire book by separating the pages on the perforated lines and keep the *Tidbits for Teachers, Energizing Explorations,* and *Great Graphs* for future reference.
- Create each game as outlined in the *Preparation* section of each direction card.
- Assemble each game board by taping the pages together. There is an illustration on each direction card showing how the completed game board will look. Mount the game board on a piece of poster board or oak tag. Cut out and mount the answer key for each game board on the back. Laminate the game board for durability.
- Cut out and laminate the picture cards and direction cards.
- Store picture cards and direction cards in resealable storage bags. Label each bag with the game name label provided in the back of this book (page 175), and attach each storage bag of game pieces to its game board.
- Organize the entire collection of board games in plastic file boxes, durable magazine/book holders, desktop file holders, or see-through plastic envelopes with button-and-string fasteners or hook and loop closures.

Push and Pull

Physical Science—Position and Motion of Objects

- The position and motion of objects can be changed by pushing or pulling.
- The size of the change is related to the strength of the push or pull.

 **Tidbits for Teachers**

Force

- Objects remain at rest unless acted upon.
- It takes a force to set something in motion.
- *Force* is any influence that changes the position and motion of an object.
- Pushes, pulls, and friction are familiar forces.
- All pushes and pulls have strength.
- Force causes acceleration. The more force exerted, the greater the acceleration.
- *Gravity* is a force that pulls objects toward the ground.
- *Air pressure* is a force exerted on people and objects by the air around us.
- *Friction* is a force caused by things rubbing together. Friction slows down and stops motion.

Energizing Exploration: Push and Pull on the Playground

Gather students for a discussion on pushing and pulling. What is the difference between the two? When do we use pushing and when do we use pulling? Have students do the following activities to experience pushing and pulling.

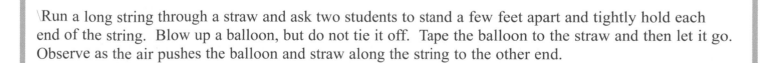

- Throw a rope over the swing set on the playground. Attach one end of the rope to a bucket and allow the students to take turns pulling on the rope to hoist the bucket into the air.
- Play a game of Tug of War with the class to experience pulling.
- Engage the students in the exercises of "push ups" and "pull ups."
- Play catch with a partner. Have the students come up with as many different ways as possible to push a ball. (Examples: Roll the ball back and forth, dribble the ball, bounce or chest pass the ball.)
- Demonstrate friction as the students push toy cars on different surfaces—grass, gravel, dirt, cement, sand, wood. Lead the students to conclude that smoother, slippery surfaces have less friction.

\Run a long string through a straw and ask two students to stand a few feet apart and tightly hold each end of the string. Blow up a balloon, but do not tie it off. Tape the balloon to the straw and then let it go. Observe as the air pushes the balloon and straw along the string to the other end.

Energizing Exploration: Brainstorm and Browse

Brainstorm with students some daily activities at home and/or school that require a push or pull and record their ideas on chart paper.

- opening the curtains—*pull*
- opening a door—*pull or push* (depending on door)
- opening a cupboard—*pull*
- opening the refrigerator—*pull*
- typing on the computer—*push*

- using a remote control—*push*
- rocking in a rocking chair—*push*
- opening the car door—*pull*
- putting on socks—*pull*
- flushing the toilet—*push*

Then browse through magazines to find and cut out pictures of items that require a push or pull in our daily lives. Have the students glue the pictures on two class posters labeled **Push** and **Pull**.

Energizing Exploration: Air Pressure Pushes

Have students roll a ping pong ball back and forth across a desk with a partner by blowing through straws. Discuss how students used air pressure to push the ball.

Use air pressure to push different objects. Blow on them with straws or a hair dryer. Test different objects to see how far they will go.

- cotton ball
- crayon
- feather
- leaf

- marker
- paper clip
- pencil
- piece of paper

- rock
- rubber ball
- toothpick

Lead a discussion about the experiment. Help students to see that the lighter the object, the further it will go. Also, objects that are round will go farther because they roll.

Energizing Exploration: Punch Card Pull

Each student will need the following items:

- a small piece of heavy paper
- a hole punch
- some yarn

Allow students to create their own design by punching holes in the paper. Tie one end of a piece of yarn onto a hole. Show students how to lace the yarn by pulling it through the holes of their design.

Energizing Exploration: Peel and Pull

Students can enjoy a variety of snacks that require a pull.

- banana
- fruit roll-up

- string cheese
- taffy

- licorice

Push and Pull

Physical Science—Position and Motion of Objects

Objective: To understand that objects are put into motion with a force known as a *push* or a *pull*. To identify a force as pushing or pulling.

Preparation

1. Remove and assemble the Push and Pull game board (pages 10 and 11). Mount the game board on poster board or oak tag and attach the answer key to the back (page 171). Laminate the game board.

2. Laminate and cut out the Push and Pull picture cards (pages 13, 15, and 17).

3. Cut out and laminate the Push and Pull Directions card (below).

4. Store the Push and Pull picture cards in a resealable storage bag. Label the bag with the game name label (page 175).

   Note: It is important to review each set of picture cards with students before playing a game. Some pictures could be interpreted in more than one way.

Push and Pull Directions

Materials

- Push and Pull game board
- Push and Pull picture cards

How to Play the Game

2–4 players

1. Shuffle the Push and Pull picture cards and place them facedown beside the game board.
2. Take turns drawing a picture card. For each card, decide which of the forces is needed, a push or a pull. Place the card in the correct box.
3. Continue taking turns until all the cards have been placed on the board.
4. Remove each stack of cards separately and check them against the answer key.

PUSH

Push
and
Pull

Push
and
Pull

Push
and
Pull

Push
and
Pull

Push
and
Pull

Push
and
Pull

Push
and
Pull

Push
and
Pull

14

Push
and
Pull

Push
and
Pull

Push
and
Pull

Push
and
Pull

Push
and
Pull

Push
and
Pull

Push
and
Pull

Push
and
Pull

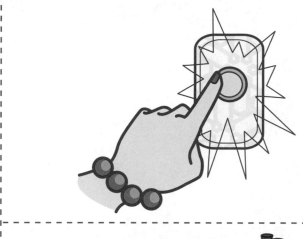

Great Graphs

Picture Graph

Using the picture cards from the Push and Pull game, have students work cooperatively to graph the picture cards according to the type of force they display—a *push* or a *pull*. Students could use a pocket chart or floor graph to graph the cards or just arrange them on a table or on the floor.

When the graph is completed, discuss the results with students.

Answer Key—page 171

Independent Graph

Make a copy for each student of the Push and Pull Graphing Sheet and Graphing Picture Cards on pages 19 and 20. Have students cut apart the picture cards, then glue the picture cards on the graphing sheet to show the type of force they display—a *push* or a *pull*.

This exercise can be used as an assessment tool.

Answer Key—page 171

10		
9		
8		
7		
6		
5		
4		
3		
2		
1		
	Push	Pull

Push
and
Pull

Push
and
Pull

Push
and
Pull

Push
and
Pull

10		
9		
8		
7		
6		
5		
4		
3		
2		
1		
	Push	Pull

Sink or Float

Physical Science—Properties of Objects and Materials

- Objects have many observable properties.
- Properties can be used to sort a group of objects.

 **Tidbits for Teachers**

Sink: To go down to the bottom; submerge; to fall or drop to a lower level; the opposite of float

Float: To remain on the surface of a liquid; the opposite of sink

- Things made of wood usually float and things made of metal usually sink.

- Children tend to assume that weight and size affect whether objects sink or float, regardless of material. (Big, heavy objects sink. Small, light objects float.) This is not always the case.
  Examples: A basketball is big and floats. A giant tree trunk floats. A penny is small and sinks. A grain of sand sinks.

- Changing the shape of an object affects whether it sinks or floats.

- The type of liquid an object is in affects whether it sinks or floats. Fresh water is less dense than salt water, so some objects that float in salt water will sink in fresh water.

Energizing Exploration: Sink or Float Aquarium

To introduce the concepts of sink and float, gather the students together to conduct an exploration. Fill a glass aquarium or a large bowl with water. Have students predict whether each object will sink or float, then place it in the water to test their prediction.

Note: The same objects appear on the picture cards in the Sink or Float game.

apple	key	rock
birthday candle	leaf	rubber band
button	marbles	soap
clothespin	paper	sponge
coins	paper clip	toothbrush
cork	pencil	twig
grapes	craft stick	

Energizing Exploration: Sink or Float Stations

Divide the class into three groups. Each group will visit three stations that you have set up around the room to investigate the buoyancy of objects. Make a copy for each student of the Observation Journal (pages 23 and 24) so that the students can record their findings. After each group has had the opportunity to visit all 3 stations, bring the class back together to share and discuss their findings.

Station 1

Bath Buddies

- bar of soap
- rubber ducky
- sponge
- bucket of water
- wash cloth
- shampoo

Station 2

School Supplies

- pencil
- scissors
- glue stick
- crayon
- eraser
- bucket of water

Station 3

Balls

- beach ball
- soccer ball
- wiffle ball
- golf ball
- baseball
- bucket of water

Energizing Exploration: Float Your Boat

Provide each student with a piece of aluminum foil. Show students how to shape a boat with the foil. Place three or four tubs of water around the room. Have each student place his or her boat in the water to observe that it floats. Give each student a handful of pennies. Tell the students to place the pennies one by one into the boat. Count the number of pennies it takes to sink the boat. Record the amount it took to sink each student's boat. Compare the results.

Energizing Exploration: Clay Creations

Set out three or four tubs of water around the room. Give students modeling clay or play clay and show them how to form a ball. Let students test their clay balls in a tub of water to see if they sink or float. (They should sink.) Now, ask the students to change the shape of their modeling clay to create something that will float. Follow up with the students as to what shapes they found would sink and what shapes they found would float.

Energizing Exploration: Super Salt Water

Have your students work in teams of two to discover that an egg sinks in fresh water but floats in salt water. Each pair of students will need the following items:

- 2 clear plastic cups with water
- 2 eggs
- salt
- a spoon

Instruct the students to place an egg in one cup of water and observe how it sinks to the bottom. Now, tell the students to put the other egg in the second cup. Have them add one spoonful of salt at a time until the egg floats to the top.

Sink or Float

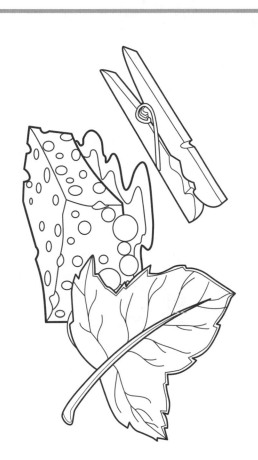

_____'s

Observation Journal

It floats!

It sinks!

It floats!

It sinks!

It floats!

It sinks!

Sink or Float

Physical Science—Properties of Objects and Materials

Objective: To predict, observe, and classify objects according to whether they sink or float in water.

Preparation

1. Remove and assemble the Sink or Float game board (pages 28 and 29). Mount the game board on poster board or oak tag and attach the answer key to the back (page 171). Laminate the game board.

2. Laminate and cut out the Sink or Float picture cards (pages 31, 33, and 35).

3. Cut out and laminate the Sink or Float Directions card (below).

4. Store the Sink or Float picture cards in a resealable storage bag. Label the bag with the game name label (page 175).

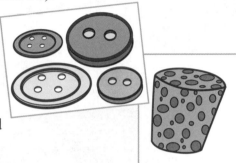

Note: It is important to review each set of picture cards with students before playing a game. Some pictures could be interpreted in more than one way.

Sink or Float Directions

Materials

- Sink or Float game board
- Sink or Float picture cards

How to Play the Game

2–4 players

1. Shuffle the Sink or Float picture cards and place them facedown beside the game board.

2. Take turns drawing a picture card. For each card, decide if the object will sink or float in water. Place the card in the correct box.

3. Continue taking turns until all the cards have been placed on the board.

4. Remove each stack of cards separately and check them against the answer key.

FLOAT

Sink
or
Float

Sink
or
Float

Sink
or
Float

Sink
or
Float

Sink
or
Float

Sink
or
Float

Sink
or
Float

Sink
or
Float

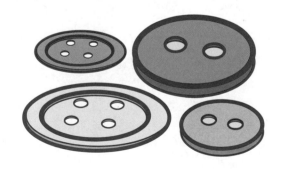

Sink

or

Float

Sink

or

Float

Sink

or

Float

Sink

or

Float

Sink

or

Float

Sink

or

Float

Sink

or

Float

Sink

or

Float

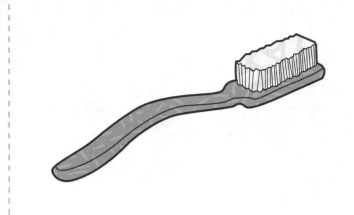
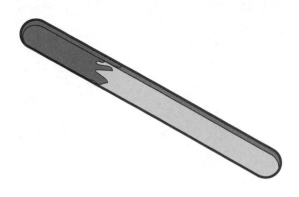
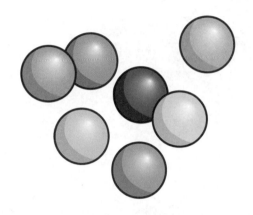
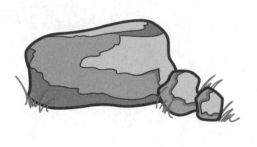

Great Graphs

Picture Graph

Using the picture cards from the game Sink or Float, have students work cooperatively to graph the picture cards according to whether they sink or float. Students could use a pocket chart or floor graph to graph the cards or just arrange them on a table or on the floor.

When the graph is completed, discuss the results with students.

Answer Key—page 171

Independent Graph

Make a copy for each student of the Sink or Float Graphing Sheet and Graphing Picture Cards on pages 37 and 38. Have students cut apart the pictur cards, then glue the picture cards on the graphing sheet to show whether each object *sinks* or *floats*.

This exercise can be used as an assessment tool.

Answer Key—page 171

	Sink	Float
10		
9		
8		
7		
6		
5	🪨	
4	📎	🍃
3	⚬⚬	╱
2	🔑	📄
1	⚬⚬	🗑
	Sink	Float

Sink
or
Float

Sink
or
Float

Sink
or
Float

Sink
or
Float

10		
9		
8		
7		
6		
5		
4		
3		
2		
1		
	Sink	Float

Mighty Materials

Physical Science—Properties of Objects and Materials

- Materials are substances used to make objects.
- An object is a visible and tangible thing. Objects are made of one or more materials.
- Materials can be natural or human-made.

 **Tidbits for Teachers**

Metals

- Metals are found in the ground.
- Metals are hard, strong, and often shiny.
- Metals do not break easily.
- Metal is popular for making coins, silverware, instruments, hangers, cooking pots, etc.

Wood

- Wood comes from trees.
- Wood is strong and lightweight.
- Wood is flexible and long lasting.
- Wood is popular for making boats, homes, furniture, fences, doors, pencils, etc.

Paper

- Paper is made from wood.
- Paper is thin but tough.
- Paper is recyclable.
- Paper is popular for making gift wrap, notepads, envelopes, sacks, maps, etc.

Energizing Exploration: Brown Bag Bracket

Divide the class into three groups. Provide each group with a brown bag of different metal, wood, and paper objects. Allow students to explore the objects in their bag. Then ask the groups to sort the objects by any attribute they can think of. Allow each group to share how they sorted. Continue sorting until a group sorts their objects by metal, wood, and paper. Ask each group to then sort their objects by metal, wood, and paper. Compile a list of the objects on a large group poster under the headings **Metal**, **Wood**, and **Paper**.

Energizing Exploration: Observation Journals

Copy the Mighty Materials Observation Page (pages 40–42) for each student. Ask students to search the classroom and playground for things made of metal, paper, and wood and record them on their observation pages. Use the students' pages to create three class books: Things Made of Wood, Things Made of Metal, and Things Made of Paper.

Metal

Wood

Paper

Mighty Materials

Physical Science—Properties of Objects and Materials

Objectives: To identify the material (wood, paper, metal) that an object is made of. To sort a group of objects by the materials from which the objects are made.

Preparation

1. Remove and assemble the Mighty Materials game board (pages 46, 47, and 49). Mount the game board on poster board or oak tag and attach the answer key to the back (page 171). Laminate the game board.

2. Laminate and cut out the Mighty Materials picture cards (pages 51, 53, and 55).

3. Cut out and laminate the Mighty Materials Directions card (below).

4. Store the Mighty Materials picture cards in a resealable storage bag. Label the bag with the game name label (page 175).

Note: It is important to review each set of picture cards with students before playing a game. Some pictures could be interpreted in more than one way.

Mighty Materials Directions

Materials

- Mighty Materials game board
- Mighty Materials picture cards

How to Play the Game

2–4 players

1. Shuffle the Mighty Materials picture cards and place them facedown beside the game board.

2. Take turns drawing a picture card. For each card, identify the material the object is made of—wood, metal, or paper. Place the card in the correct box.

3. Continue taking turns until all the cards have been placed on the mats.

4. Remove each stack of cards and check them against the answer key.

PAPER

METAL

50

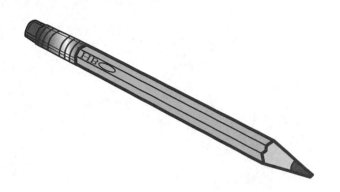

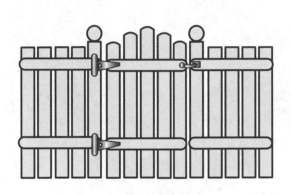

Mighty
Materials

Mighty
Materials

Mighty
Materials

Mighty
Materials

Mighty
Materials

Mighty
Materials

Mighty
Materials

Mighty
Materials

Mighty
Materials

Mighty
Materials

Mighty
Materials

Mighty
Materials

Mighty
Materials

Mighty
Materials

Mighty
Materials

Mighty
Materials

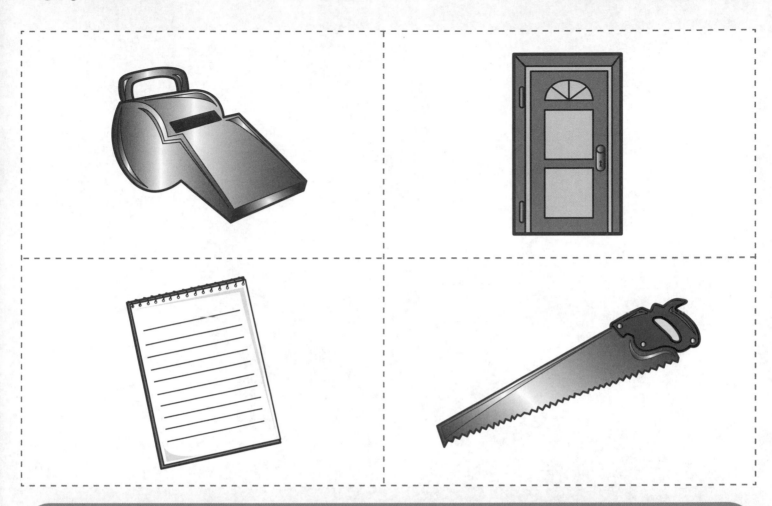

Great Graphs

Grab Bag Graph

Prior to this activity, gather a collection of objects made of metal, wood, and paper. (Examples: paper clip, key, spoon, small metal can, book, grocery sack, seed packet, note card, napkin, dollar bill, craft stick, pencil, wooden puzzle piece, building block, tongue depressor.) Place the objects into a grab bag. Students take turns pulling an object from the bag and placing it on a floor graph by material (wood, metal, or paper).

When the graph is completed, discuss the results with students.

Picture Graph

Using the picture cards from the game Mighty Materials, have students work cooperatively to graph the picture cards according to whether they are made of wood, metal, or paper. Students could use a pocket chart or floor graph to graph the cards or just arrange them on a table or on the floor.

When the graph is completed, discuss the results with students.

Answer Key—page 171

Independent Graph

Make a copy for each student of the Mighty Materials Graphing Sheet and Graphing Picture Cards on pages 57 and 58.

Have students cut apart the picture cards, then glue the picture cards on the graphing sheet to show whether they are made of wood, metal, or paper. This exercise can be used as an assessment tool.

Answer Key—page 171

Mighty
Materials

Mighty
Materials

Mighty
Materials

Mighty
Materials

10			
9			
8			
7			
6			
5			
4			
3			
2			
1			
	Wood	Metal	Paper

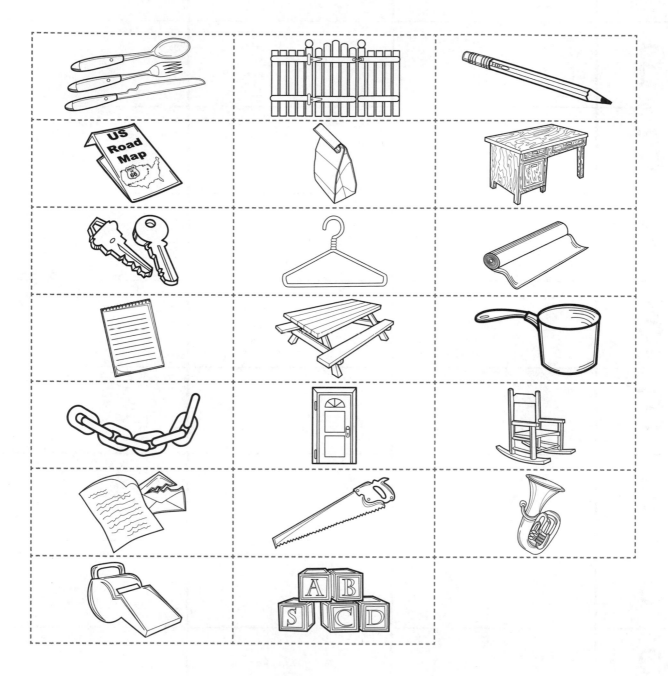

Winter Ways

Earth and Space Science—Changes in the Earth and Sky

- Weather changes from day to day and over the seasons, affecting Earth and its inhabitants.

 **Tidbits for Teachers**

Migration

- *Migration* is the movement of animals in search of a better food source or climate, or to reproduce. Changes in temperature, scarcity of food, and an increase in appetite triggers an animal to prepare for migration. Before migrating, animals must increase their body fat in order to have plenty of energy for their long journey.
- Migration movements are from one area to another and back again and tend to correspond with the seasons. Migrating can be done by walking, flying, swimming, etc.
- Some animals migrate a short way while others travel many miles. The arctic tern makes the longest migration— over 21,000 miles. It flies from the Arctic to the Antarctic and back again. The monarch butterfly migrates from Canada and the northern United States down to Central Mexico.
- The sun, stars, moon, Earth's magnetic field, and geographic features aid the migration of animals.
- Grazing animals such as zebra, wildebeest, buffalo, and antelope migrate in herds.
- Some animals migrate by day and some animals migrate by night. Migrating animals use the same path every year.
- Whales, seals, sea turtles, and fish migrate in water. The gray whale is the longest migrating mammal.
- Sea turtles migrate to lay their eggs on sandy beaches.
- Butterflies, moths, aphids, locusts, dragonflies are a few of the insects that migrate. Whole colonies of army ants migrate every night.

Hibernation

- *Hibernation* is a state of inactivity or a deep sleep.
- Hibernating animals slow their breathing and heart beat to conserve energy. They do not move or get rid of body wastes. Stored body fat provides hibernating animals with the energy necessary to survive.
- Hibernating animals choose safe places away from enemies to sleep. Quiet and darkness are important. Animals that hibernate find shelter for the winter in underground burrows, dens, caves, and the bottoms of lakes.
- An animal's body temperature drops to a temperature that is similar to the surrounding environment. If temperatures drop below freezing in an animal's den, the animal begins to shiver which warms the animal up, but also uses some of its stored fat.
- Hibernating animals (skunks, opossums, badgers, raccoons, beavers, squirrels, bears) may wake for short periods.
- Warm-blooded animals that hibernate include groundhogs, bats, and hamsters.
- Cold-blooded animals that hibernate include snakes, frogs, toads, lizards, and turtles.
- Ladybugs, mosquitoes, and bumblebees are a few hibernating insects.

Adaptation (staying awake and active)

- Some animals remain in their environment and stay active during winter. To survive they must be able to find water, food, and shelter to stay warm.
- Some animals grow thicker fur, store up layers of fat, gather and store food, snuggle together, hide under rocks, leaves, logs, and in trees, and use camouflage to stay safe.
- Snowshoe rabbits and weasels turn from brown to white to blend in with the snow.

Energizing Exploration: Hooray for Hibernation

Discuss how animals that hibernate store up body fat and grow thicker fur to stay warm. A hibernating mammal's body temperature is around 43 degrees Fahrenheit.

Set out a container of ice water. Allow students to feel the coldness. Then conduct a "blubber" experiment to show how stored fat insulates an animal's body. You will need a tub of ice water, vegetable shortening in plastic bags, and sanitary gloves for each student. Have each student put on a sanitary glove. Place his or her hand into a bag of vegetable shortening—the "blubber." Set the bag into the container of ice water. The students will feel that the "blubber" keeps their hand warm.

* Create a "Hibernation Hide Out" in the classroom for students to crawl inside for some quiet story time.
* Have a "Hibernation Hour" where students can bring pillows and blankets and hibernate for a short time.

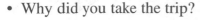

Energizing Exploration: Camouflage Connection

Discuss how many animals use camouflage to adapt for the winter. Go outside and scatter a box of multi-colored toothpicks in a grassy area. Give the students 30 seconds to pick up as many toothpicks as possible. Discuss which colors of toothpicks they were able to find easily and which colors were difficult to find and why.

Energizing Exploration: Awesome Adaptations

Discuss all the ways that humans adapt for the winter.

- We bundle up in warm clothes. We wear hats, gloves, coats, jackets, boots, mittens, and scarves.

- We use fireplaces and heaters.

- We drink warm drinks such as hot chocolate!

Talk about any vacations that the students have taken where the weather was better than at home. Explain that this is one of the reasons that birds migrate. Compare their trips to animal migration. Plot on a map the places the students have traveled. Use the following questions to lead the discussion.

- Why did you take the trip?
- Did you plan ahead?
- How did you find your way to your destination?

- Did you make the trip all in one day?
- Where did you stay overnight?
- Did you stop and eat?

Compare the students' answers to the ways in which animals migrate.

Winter Ways

Earth and Space Science—Changes in the Earth and Sky

Objective: To identify animals which survive the winter by hibernating, migrating, or staying awake and active (adapting).

Preparation

1. Remove and assemble the Winter Ways game board (pages 63, 65, and 67). Mount the game board on poster board or oak tag and attach the answer key to the back (page 171). Laminate the game board.

2. Laminate and cut out the Winter Ways picture cards (pages 69, 71, and 73).

3. Cut out and laminate the Winter Ways Directions card (below).

4. Store the Winter Ways picture cards in a resealable storage bag. Label the bag with the game name label (page 175).

Note: It is important to review each set of picture cards with students before playing a game. Some pictures could be interpreted in more than one way.

Winter Ways Directions

Materials

- Winter Ways game board
- Winter Ways picture cards

How to Play the Game

2–4 players

1. Shuffle the Winter Ways picture cards and place them facedown beside the game board.

2. Take turns drawing a picture card. For each card, decide which way the animal survives winter—*hibernate*, *migrate*, or *stay awake*. Place the card in the correct box.

3. Continue taking turns until all the cards have been placed on the board.

4. Remove each stack of cards separately and check them against the answer key.

Migrate

Stay Awake

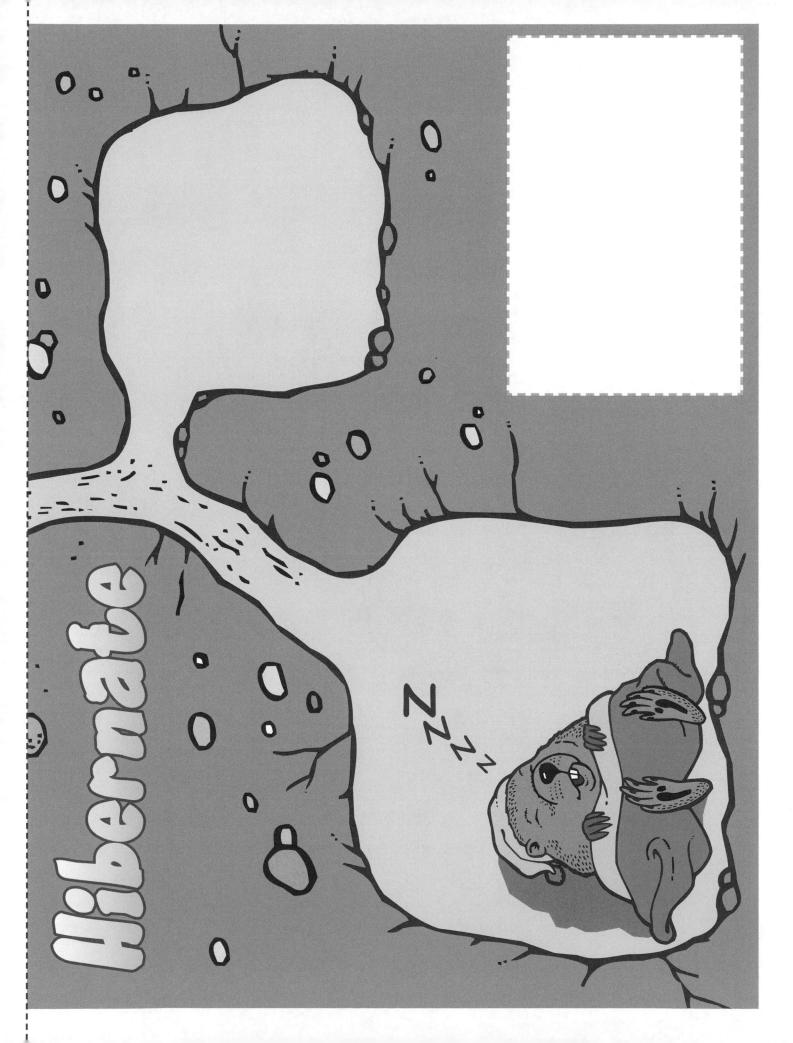

Brown Bat

Canadian Goose

Snowshoe Rabbit

Weasel

Frog

Monarch Butterfly

Gray Whale

Turtle

Winter
Ways

Winter
Ways

Winter
Ways

Winter
Ways

Winter
Ways

Winter
Ways

Winter
Ways

Winter
Ways

Fox

Snake

Robin

Deer

Groundhog

Dragonfly

Snowy Owl

Ladybird Beetle

Winter
Ways

Winter
Ways

Winter
Ways

Winter
Ways

Winter
Ways

Winter
Ways

Winter
Ways

Winter
Ways

Crow

Wolf

Chipmunk

Turkey

Great Graphs

Picture Graph

Using the picture cards from the game Winter Ways, have students work cooperatively to graph the picture cards according to the way each animal survives winter—hibernate, migrate, or adapt (stay awake and active). Students could use a pocket chart or floor graph to graph the cards or just arrange them on a table or on the floor.

When the graph is completed, discuss the results with students.

Answer Key—page 171

Independent Graph

Make a copy for each student of the Winter Ways Graphing Sheet and Graphing Picture Cards on pages 75 and 76. Have students cut apart the picture cards, then glue the picture cards on the graphing sheet to show the ways animals survive winter—*hibernate, migrate,* or *adapt* (stay awake and active).

This exercise can be used as an assessment tool.

Answer Key—page 171

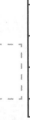

	Hibernate	Migrate	Adapt
10			
9			
8			
7			
6			
5			🐰
4		🐋	🐺
3	🐸	🦋	🦊
2	🦇	🐦	🦅
1	🐢	🦋	🦊

Winter
Ways

Winter
Ways

Winter
Ways

Winter
Ways

10			
9			
8			
7			
6			
5			
4			
3			
2			
1			
	Hibernate	Migrate	Adapt

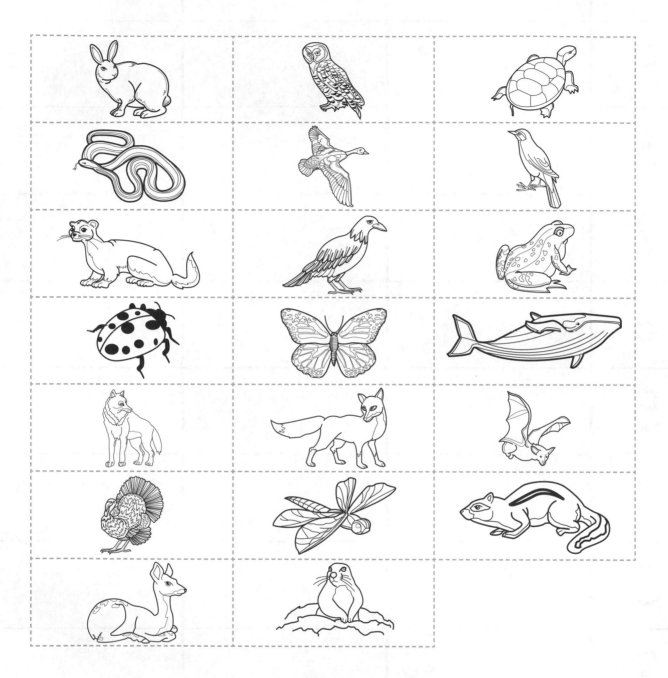

Tempting Temperatures

Earth and Space Science—Changes in the Earth and Sky

- Weather can be described by measurable quantities, such as temperature.

 ### Tidbits for Teachers

Climate: Climate is the average weather in a specific location observed and recorded over a given period of time. Climate is useful for forecasting the weather.

Temperature: Temperature is the measurement of how fast or slow molecules move. Slow moving molecules mean a cold temperature. Fast moving molecules mean a hot temperature.

- Climates can be hot, cold, dry, or wet and differ from place to place. The United States is divided into seven regional climate areas.

- Weather refers to the events that happen in the atmosphere on a daily basis—rain, snow, lightning, etc.

- Meteorologists are scientists who observe, record, and predict weather.

- The amount of sunlight affects the temperature of an area. Daytime usually has higher temperatures than nighttime. Clouds can keep the temperature cooler by blocking some heat from the sun.

- Temperatures over water are cooler than temperatures over land.

- Areas close to the equator have hot temperatures. Areas close to the North and South Poles are cold.

- A thermometer is the tool for measuring temperature. Temperature is measured in degrees. Two scales for measuring temperature are Fahrenheit and Celsius.

- Adjectives that describe temperature include *hot, cold, warm, cool, chilly, boiling,* and *freezing.*

- Temperature affects our daily activities—the amount of food we eat, the kind of liquid we drink, where and when we exercise, and the type of clothes we wear.

Energizing Exploration: Suitcase Sort

To introduce the topic of hot and cold temperatures, gather the students together to do a class sorting activity. You will need a bag filled with the following items:

- bathing suit
- beach ball
- beach towel
- boots
- coat
- gloves

- mittens
- shorts
- stocking cap
- suntan lotion
- sunglasses

- sweater
- tank top
- turtleneck
- winter scarf
- wool socks

Label two suitcases, one for hot climates and one for cold climates, and set them on the floor. Allow the students to each take a turn pulling an item out of the bag and packing it in the correct suitcase.

Energizing Exploration: Weather Wonderings

There are so many different ways to find out what the weather is going to be like outside. Teach your students to use as many different resources as possible to find out their daily weather.

- Locate the weather section of a newspaper and find out what the predicted temperature is for that day.
- Go to an Internet weather site to find out what the temperature is in different cities.
- Ask students to predict tomorrow's weather. Record their predictions and check them the next day.

Record the daily temperature using the graph on page 83. Collect and record data for several weeks then compare graphs and look for trends.

Energizing Exploration: Weather Reports

Ask each student to take a day to report the weather to the class. This will require students to do a little at-home research the night before their big day. Copy the parent letter and Weather Reporter's Fact Sheet on pages 81 and 82 for each student. This will help them to know what type of information they should report to the class. Let the weather reporter wear a blazer and give him or her a pointer to make him or her look official. Use an interactive weather bulletin board as a back drop.

Energizing Exploration: Climate Classifications

As a class, brainstorm and record on a class chart everything students can think of for hot climates and cold climates. Ask the students the following questions:

1. What activities do you participate in?
2. What do you wear?
3. What different foods and drinks do we associate with each type of climate?
4. When you are hot, what types of things do you do to cool down?
5. When you are cold, what types of things do you do to warm up?

Copy the Climate Classification sheets (pages 79 and 80) for each student. Allow the students to draw a picture of their favorite things to do in each type of climate. Then ask the students to write a word or a sentence to describe what they are doing in their picture. Compile the students' work into a class book.

Energizing Exploration: Temperature Testers

Pre-label the thermometers on page 84 with school locations such as the gym, the playground, the school cafeteria, the nurse's office, or a hallway and make copies. Show students how to read a thermometer to the nearest ten degrees, then divide students into pairs or small groups and give each group a thermometer. Have each group take its thermometer to one of the specified locations and record the temperature by coloring in the correct temperature reading with a red crayon. Back in class, have students compare and discuss their findings.

Hot

Cold

Date: _____

Dear Parents,

In conjunction with our study of hot and cold temperatures we are going to let each student have a turn being our weather reporter! The pre-assigned date that your child will report the weather is written below. On the night before or the morning of your child's assigned day, please watch the news or look in the newspaper to find out the information that your child will need. Your child is not expected to have the exact facts updated the minute school begins—the information that you get from the news the night before is fine.

Assist your child in filling out the Weather Reporter's Fact Sheet which he or she can use to give the report. It would be helpful if you would help your child practice giving the weather report a couple of times so that he/she is comfortable being the weather reporter.

Happy weather watching!

_____ will be the weather reporter on
(child's name)

the morning of _____.
(date)

Thank you for your help,

_____

And now . . . today's weather!

The date today is _____

The temperature today will be _____

The weather today will be _____

Sunny　　　　　　　　　　**Cloudy**

Snowy　　　　　　　　　　**Rainy**

Today would be a good day to

_____

_____

Weather Wonderings

Daily Outdoor Temperatures

	Monday	Tuesday	Wednesday	Thursday	Friday
100					
95					
90					
85					
80					
75					
70					
65					
60					
55					
50					
45					
40					
35					
30					
25					
20					
15					
10					
5					

Temperature Testers

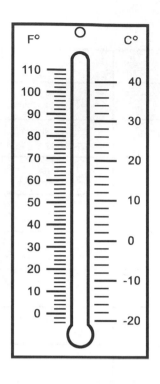

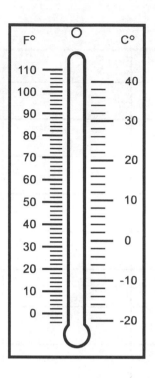

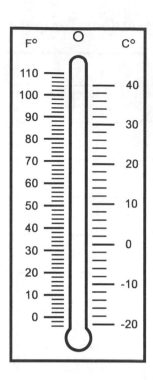

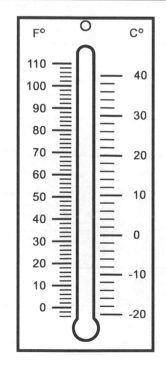

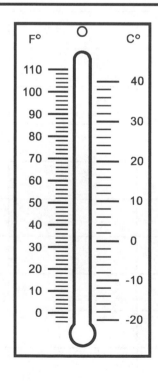

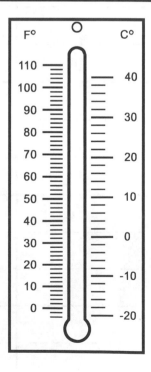

Tempting Temperatures

Earth and Space Science—Changes in the Earth and Sky

Objective: To classify temperatures as hot or cold.

Preparation

1. Remove and assemble the Tempting Temperatures game board (pages 88 and 89). Mount the game board on poster board or oak tag and attach the answer key to the back (page 172). Laminate the game board.

2. Laminate and cut out the Tempting Temperatures picture cards (pages 91, 93, and 95).

3. Cut out and laminate the Tempting Temperatures Directions card (below).

4. Store the Tempting Temperatures picture cards in a resealable storage bag. Label the bag with the game name label (page 175).

Note: It is important to review the set of picture cards with students before playing a game. Some pictures could be interpreted in more than one way.

Tempting Temperatures Directions

Materials

- Tempting Temperatures game board
- Tempting Temperatures picture cards

How to Play the Game

2–4 players

1. Shuffle the Tempting Temperatures picture cards and place them facedown beside the game board.

2. Take turns drawing a picture card. For each card, decide in which temperature the object or activity would be most appropriate—*hot* or *cold*. Place the card in the correct box.

3. Continue taking turns until all the cards have been placed on the board.

4. Remove each stack of cards separately and check them against the answer key.

86

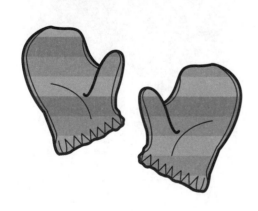

Tempting
Temperatures

Tempting
Temperatures

Tempting
Temperatures

Tempting
Temperatures

Tempting
Temperatures

Tempting
Temperatures

Tempting
Temperatures

Tempting
Temperatures

Tempting
Temperatures

Tempting
Temperatures

Tempting
Temperatures

Tempting
Temperatures

Tempting
Temperatures

Tempting
Temperatures

Tempting
Temperatures

Tempting
Temperatures

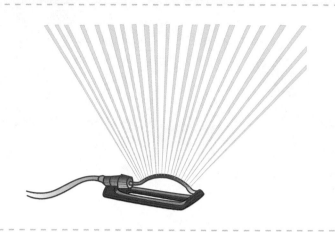

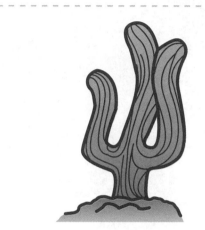

Great Graphs

Picture Graph

Using the picture cards from the game Tempting Temperatures, have students work cooperatively to graph the picture cards according to the temperature represented—hot or cold. Students could use a pocket chart or floor graph to graph the cards or just arrange them on a table or on the floor.

When the graph is completed, discuss the results with students.

Answer Key—page 172

Independent Graph

Make a copy for each student of the Tempting Temperatures Graphing Sheet and Graphing Picture Cards on pages 97 and 98. Have students cut apart the picture cards then glue the picture cards on the graphing sheet to show whether they represent hot or cold.

This exercise can be used as an assessment tool.

Answer Key—page 172

	Hot	Cold
10		
9		
8		
7		
6	🥤	
5	💦	☕
4	🏊	⛄
3	👙	🧤
2	🧴	🛖
1	☀️	🧊
	Hot	Cold

Tempting
Temperatures

Tempting
Temperatures

Tempting
Temperatures

Tempting
Temperatures

10		
9		
8		
7		
6		
5		
4		
3		
2		
1		
	Hot	Cold

Night and Day

Earth and Space Science—Objects in the Sky

- The sun, moon, and stars are natural objects in the sky.

Changes in the Earth and Sky

- Objects in the sky have patterns of movement that can be observed and described.

- The sun appears to move across the sky in the same way every day.

 **Tidbits for Teachers**

Night and Day

- Day and night are caused by the rotation of the Earth. One half of the Earth is always light while the other half is dark.

- The portion of the Earth facing the sun has daytime. The portion of the Earth away from the sun has night. It is the Earth's own shadow which makes night.

- The Earth makes one full rotation every 24 hours.

- *Daytime* is from sunrise to sunset. *Nighttime* is from sunset to sunrise.

- Every day starts at midnight.

- *Equinox* is the time when days and nights are the same length (around March 21st and September 21st).

- *Solstice* is the time when day or night is the longest it will be (around June 21st and December 20th).

- During the day we see the sun in different places in the sky. In the morning, the sun appears in the east.

- At noon, we see the sun directly overhead. In the afternoon, the sun sets in the west.

   Day and Night Vocabulary: sunrise, day, noon, spin, rotate, sunset, night, dawn, dusk, midnight, revolve

---

Energizing Exploration: Day and Night Demonstration

Model day and night for your students. Use a lamp to represent the sun and a student to represent the Earth. Shine the light on the student and have the student spin slowly, demonstrating the rotation of the Earth. When the student is facing the lamp it is daytime. When the student's back is toward the lamp it is night.

Allow the students to create their own day and night demonstration using a flashlight and an orange placed on a pencil. Put a small sticker or pin on one side of the orange to represent your city or town. Have the students slowly spin the orange and shine the flashlight on it. Ask students to tell whether your town is having day or night as the orange rotates.

Energizing Exploration: Rotate and Revolve

To better understand the meaning of *rotate* and *revolve*, have students act them out in the classroom. Place a lamp in the middle of the room. Ask the students to stand around the lamp. Have the students experience rotation by standing in place and spinning around. Have the students experience revolution by walking in a circle around the lamp. Students can rotate and revolve, just like the Earth by spinning as they walk around the lamp. **Note:** To keep dizziness to a minimum, tell students to rotate and revolve very slowly!

Energizing Exploration: Day and Night Book

Give each student a sheet of paper. Ask him or her to draw something he or she likes to do during the day on one side and something he or she likes to do at night on the other side. Have students dictate a caption for each picture. Bind their pages into *Our Day and Night Book* for the class to read.

Energizing Exploration: Make a Sundial

In the morning, take students outside and place a large sheet of paper in a sunny area on the grass. Weight each corner down so the paper will not blow away. Push a pencil or dowel through the center of the paper and into the grass so it stands upright. Ask a student to trace the shadow of the stick onto the paper. Write the time of day at the end point of the shadow. Come back each hour during the day to trace the shadow as it moves on the paper and record the time. At the end of the day, discuss the results with students. Why did the shadow move?

Energizing Exploration: Nighttime Walk

Ask the students to take a walk in the dark one evening with their family. Ask them to look for things that they don't see during the day. Tell them to bring a flashlight to look for nighttime animals and to listen for unfamiliar sounds. Ask students to tell the class about what they experienced on their nighttime walks.

Energizing Exploration: Night in the Daytime

Tell students that you are going to have nighttime during the day! Allow students to wear their pajamas to school and bring a favorite stuffed animal. Serve a "bedtime" snack, such as milk and cookies, and read bedtime stories. Read books and talk about nocturnal animals, community workers who work at night, and nighttime fears. At the end of the day, tell everyone goodnight!

Night and Day

Earth and Space Science—Objects in the Sky

Objective: To identify whether an object is usually used at night or in the daytime.

Preparation

1. Remove and assemble the Night and Day game board (pages 104 and 105). Mount the game board on poster board or oak tag and attach the answer key to the back (page 172). Laminate the game board.

2. Laminate and cut out the Night and Day picture cards (pages 107, 109, and 111).

3. Cut out and laminate the Night and Day Directions card (below).

4. Store the Night and Day picture cards in a resealable storage bag. Label the bag with the game name label (page 175).

   Note: It is important to review each set of picture cards with students before playing a game. Some pictures could be interpreted in more than one way.

Night and Day Directions

Materials

- Night and Day game board
- Night and Day picture cards

How to Play the Game

2–4 players

1. Shuffle the Night and Day picture cards and place them facedown beside the game board.

2. Take turns drawing a picture card. For each card, decide if it is something you would use mainly in the daytime, mainly in the nighttime, or in both the daytime and the nighttime. Place the card in the correct box.

3. Continue taking turns until all the cards have been placed on the board.

4. Remove each stack of cards separately and check them against the answer key.

NIGHT

DAY

Night
and
Day

Night
and
Day

Night
and
Day

Night
and
Day

Night
and
Day

Night
and
Day

Night
and
Day

Night
and
Day

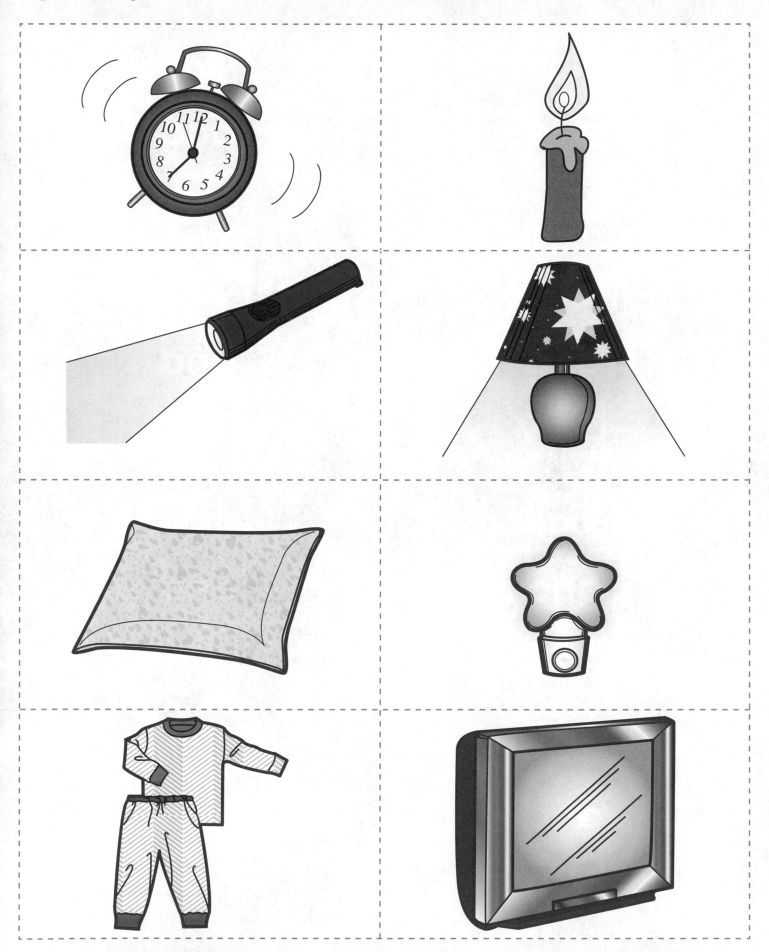

Night
and
Day

Night
and
Day

Night
and
Day

Night
and
Day

Night
and
Day

Night
and
Day

Night
and
Day

Night
and
Day

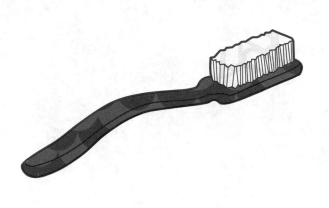

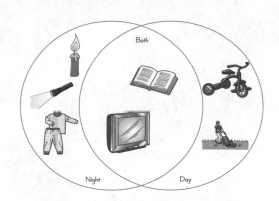

Great Graphs

Picture Graph

Using the picture cards from the game Night and Day, have students work cooperatively using a Venn diagram to sort the picture cards according to whether they are daytime activities, nighttime activities, or both. Students could use two large overlapping hula hoops on the floor to graph the cards or arrange them on a table or on the floor.

When the graph is completed, discuss the results with students.

Answer Key—page 172

Independent Graph

Make a copy for each student of the Night and Day Graphing Sheet and Graphing Picture Cards on pages 113 and 114. Have students cut apart the picture cards, then glue the picture cards on the Venn diagram. This exercise can be used as an assessment tool.

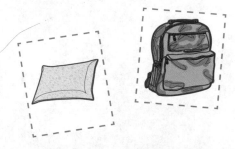

Answer Key—page 172

Night
and
Day

Night
and
Day

Night
and
Day

Night
and
Day

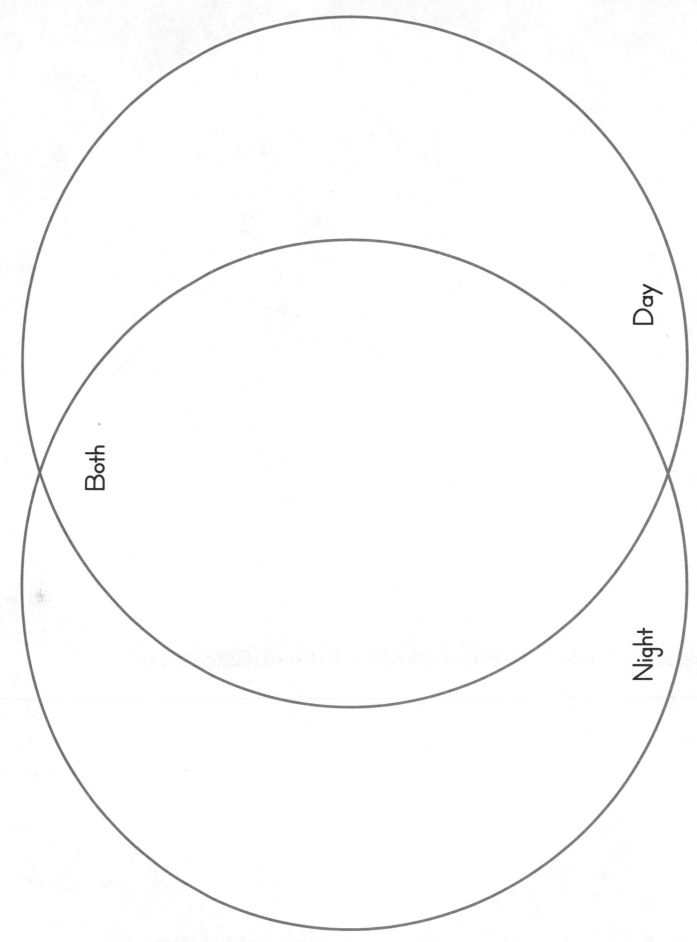

Playground Pleasures

Life Science—Characteristics of Organisms

- Children's ideas about the characteristics of organisms develop from basic concepts of living and non-living.

 ## Tidbits for Teachers

Living

- All living things need water, food, and air (oxygen).
- All living things have a circle of life—birth, growth, reproduction, and death.
- Living things must have all of the following characteristics:

    * be made of cells   * grow and change   * obtain and use energy (eat food)

    * breathe   * reproduce   * react to their environment

- Some living things can move on their own.
- All living things eventually die.
- *Biology* is the study of living things.
- All animals and plants are living things.

    Examples: ant, starfish, tree, bear, bird, mushrooms

Non-living

- Non-living things cannot move on their own or grow.

    Examples: sand, wood, glass, gold, water

- Non-living things do not eat or reproduce.
- Non-living things may exhibit one or more living characteristics but not all.

    Examples: Clouds move and change but are non-living. Water moves, changes, and reacts to the environment but is non-living. Fire needs oxygen, has energy, grows, and changes, but is non-living.

Energizing Exploration: Grab Bag Sort

Gather the students together to classify items as living or non-living. You will need a bag with the following items:

- beans
- buttons
- chalk
- coins
- erasers
- feathers

- leaves
- paper clips
- pencils
- pictures of animals
- pictures of people
- pictures of plants

- plastic animals
- plastic bottle caps
- rocks
- seashells
- washers
- wood

Use colored tape to create a two-column graph on the floor. Label one side **Living** and the other side **Non-living**. Allow one student at a time to pick an item out of the bag and decide if the item is living or non-living. Have the student place the object in its appropriate place on the floor graph. Continue until each student has had a turn or until all the items have been graphed.

Energizing Exploration: Magazine Hunt

Give each student a magazine. Let each student cut out one picture. After each student has found a picture, come together and let each student share the picture that he or she found. Discuss different ways that the class might sort the pictures that have been collected. With the students, sort the pictures by several of the categories given. If the attributes of *living* and *non-living* are not suggested, the teacher can sort the pictures accordingly and ask students to figure out the categories. In conclusion, have students place pictures in a bar graph on a large piece of butcher paper.

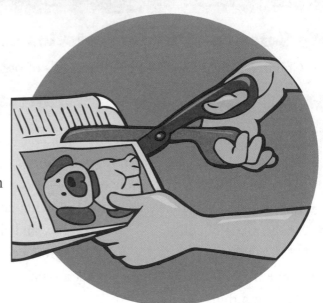

If time allows, have the students go on a magazine hunt of their own, looking for as many pictures as they can find of *living* and *non-living* objects. When they are finished, have the students use construction paper to make *living* and *non-living* picture collages.

Energizing Exploration: Scavenger Hunt

Take your class on a scavenger hunt around the playground. Allow the students to work with a partner. Have each pair walk around and collect or record ten items that they find or see, some living and some non-living. At a designated time, join back together and share what each pair found. Record all observations on chart paper. As a follow up, highlight a few selected objects and discuss the characteristics that make them living or non-living.

Note: Caution students about picking up sharp or unusual objects. Remind them not to eat anything they gather until an adult has checked it (fruits, berries or mushrooms).

Energizing Exploration: Corny Comparisons

Have fun with your class as you compare the attributes of living and non-living in pairs of objects. For example:

- Compare a real worm to a gummy worm.
- Compare a live insect in a jar to a plastic insect.
- Compare a live plant to an artificial plant.

Record the students' descriptions on chart paper or a Venn Diagram.

Playground Pleasures

Life Science—Characteristics of Organisms

Objective: To identify objects as living or non-living.

Preparation

1. Remove and assemble the Playground Pleasures game board (pages 120 and 121). Mount the game board on poster board or oak tag and attach the answer key to the back (page 172). Laminate the game board.

2. Laminate and cut out the Playground Pleasures picture cards (pages 123, 125, and 127).

3. Cut out and laminate the Playground Pleasures Directions card (below).

4. Store the Playground Pleasures picture cards in a resealable storage bag. Label the bag with the game name label (page 175).

Note: It is important to review each set of picture cards with students before playing a game. Some pictures could be interpreted in more than one way.

Playground Pleasures Directions

Materials

- Playground Pleasures game board
- Playground Pleasures picture cards

How to Play the Game

2–4 players

1. Shuffle the Playground Pleasures picture cards and place them facedown beside the game board.

2. Take turns drawing a picture card. For each card, decide if the item is living or non-living. Place the card in the correct box.

3. Continue taking turns until all the cards have been placed on the board.

4. Remove each stack of cards separately and check them against the answer key.

Living

Non-Living

Playground
Pleasures

Playground
Pleasures

Playground
Pleasures

Playground
Pleasures

Playground
Pleasures

Playground
Pleasures

Playground
Pleasures

Playground
Pleasures

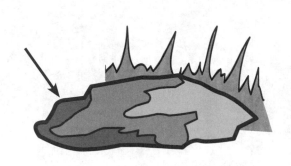

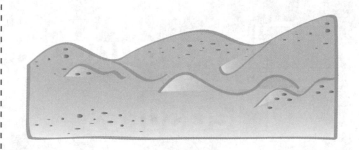

Playground
Pleasures

Playground
Pleasures

Playground
Pleasures

Playground
Pleasures

Playground
Pleasures

Playground
Pleasures

Playground
Pleasures

Playground
Pleasures

Great Graphs

Picture Graph

Using the picture cards from the game Playground Pleasures, have students work cooperatively to graph the picture cards according to whether they are living or non-living. Students could use a pocket chart or floor graph to graph the cards or just arrange them on a table or on the floor.

When the graph is completed, discuss the results with students.

Answer Key—page 172

Independent Graph

Make a copy for each student of the Playground Pleasures Graphing Sheet and Graphing Picture Cards on pages 129 and 130. Have students cut apart the picture cards, then glue the picture cards on the graphing sheet to show whether they are living or non-living.

This exercise can be used as an assessment tool.

Answer Key—page 172

Playground
Pleasures

Playground
Pleasures

Playground
Pleasures

Playground
Pleasures

	Living	Non-living
10		
9		
8		
7		
6		
5		
4		
3		
2		
1		

Leaf Litter

Life Science—Basic Needs/Features of Organisms

- Plants need air, water, nutrients, and light.
- Each plant has different structures that serve different functions in growth, survival, and reproduction.

 **Tidbits for Teachers**

Leaves

- There are two types of leafy trees—*deciduous* and *coniferous*.
- *Deciduous* trees have flat, broad leaves that change color in the fall and drop to the ground. The tree grows new leaves in the spring.
- *Coniferous* trees have needle leaves. Conifers are the world's tallest, largest, thickest, and oldest living things.
- A leaf is the part of a plant that makes food for the plant. Leaves are generally flat and thin to allow for *photosynthesis*, which is the conversion of sunlight into food.
- Leaves have different shapes, sizes, colors, and edges.
- Leaves have veins that carry water and minerals.
- *Chlorophyll* is a pigment used to absorb sunlight. It gives leaves their green color.

Simple Leaves

- A *simple leaf* is a single leaf with a bud attached to the stem.
- A simple leaf's stem is attached directly to the twig.
- Simple leaves have many shapes—oval, fan-shaped, heart-shaped, triangular.
- The leaf stem is the same as the main vein for that leaf.
- Simple leaves are very common.
    Examples: maple, oak, elm, dogwood, aspen, willow

Compound Leaves

- A *compound leaf* has two or more leaflets attached to the same leaf stem.
- The blade of a compound leaf is separated into smaller pieces.
- A compound leaflet does not have a bud on its stem.
- In spring the stem and leaflets come out of the same bud.
- In autumn the stem and leaflets fall to the ground.
    Examples: hickory, walnut, locust, ash

Needle Leaves

- Needle leaves stay green all year long.
- Needle leaves are spirally arranged.
- Needle leaves are long and thin.
- Needle leaves may live several years.
- Each year new leaves grow and the oldest leaves are shed.
    Examples: pine, spruce, hemlock, cedar, fir, juniper

Energizing Exploration: Leaf Safari

To introduce the topic of leaves, take your students on a "Leaf Safari." Go to the playground or a nearby area with lots of trees. Give students leaf collection bags and allow them to gather many different leaves. Return to the classroom and allow the students to explore the leaves in their collection bags. Guide the class as they begin to sort the leaves by different attributes. Discuss the characteristics of simple leaves, compound leaves, and needle leaves. Ask the students to then sort the leaves by these characteristics.

Make copies of the *Leaf Collection Book* on pages 133 and 134. Have students draw a picture of their favorite leaf in each category. Write a descriptive word for each chosen leaf.

Keep the collected leaves for the Lowdown on Leaves, below, and Grab Bag Graph, page 147.

Energizing Exploration: Lowdown on Leaves

- Observe leaves under a magnifying glass. Identify the veins and discuss that they carry the food to all parts of the leaf.

- Use standard and nonstandard units to measure a few of the leaves.

- Put the leaves in order from shortest to longest.

- Discuss the weight of a leaf. Have a leaf blowing race! To demonstrate how light a leaf is, use a straw to blow a leaf across a table.

Energizing Exploration: Taste Test

Have students do a taste test of the different kinds of leaves that we eat. (**Examples:** spinach, lettuce, parsley, cabbage, collards, mustard, kale.) Have the class vote on their favorite leaf to eat!

Energizing Exploration: Colorful Creations

There are so many art projects that can be done with leaves!

- Make leaf rubbings using the leaves the students collected on their Leaf Safari. Lay a leaf on the table, place a sheet of paper over it, and rub with the side of a crayon.

- Paint the underside of a leaf and press it onto paper to make a leaf print. Use different colors and many types of leaves for a beautiful effect.

- Press leaves under heavy books for a few days and use them to make note cards or placemats.

's

Leaf Collection Book

Needle Leaf

Compound Leaf

Simple Leaf

Leaf Litter

Life Science—Basic Needs/Features of Organisms

Objective: To identify leaves as compound, simple, or needle.

Preparation

1. Remove and assemble the Leaf Litter game board (pages 138, 139, and 141) and attach the answer key to the back (page 172). Laminate the game board. Mount the gameboard on poster board or oak tag.

2. Laminate and cut out the Leaf Litter picture cards (pages 143, 145, and 147).

3. Cut out and laminate the Leaf Litter Directions card (below).

4. Store the Leaf Litter picture cards in a resealable storage bag. Label the bag with the game name label (page 175).

   Note: It is important to review each set of picture cards with students before playing a game. This set of cards has been labeled to assist with leaf identification. Encourage students to use the proper name for each leaf.

Leaf Litter Directions

Materials

- Leaf Litter game board
- Leaf Litter picture cards

How to Play the Game

2–4 players

1. Shuffle the Leaf Litter picture cards and place them facedown beside the game board.

2. Take turns drawing a picture card. For each card, decide if the leaf is a compound, simple, or needle type of leaf. Place the card in the correct box.

3. Continue taking turns until all the cards have been placed on the board.

4. Remove each stack of cards separately and check them against the answer key.

SIMPLE

COMPOUND

NEEDLE

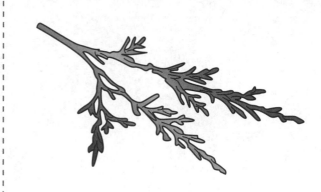

Cedar

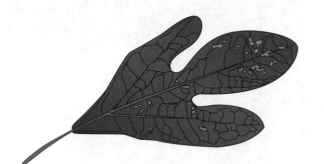

Sassafras

Buckeye

Locust

Chestnut

Ash

Douglas Fir

Redbud

Leaf
Litter

Leaf
Litter

Leaf
Litter

Leaf
Litter

Leaf
Litter

Leaf
Litter

Leaf
Litter

Leaf
Litter

Hickory

Sycamore

Black Walnut

Ginkgo

Cottonwood

Juniper

Elm

Poison Ivy

Leaf
Litter

Leaf
Litter

Leaf
Litter

Leaf
Litter

Leaf
Litter

Leaf
Litter

Leaf
Litter

Leaf
Litter

Sweet Gum

Beech

Blue Spruce

White Pine

Great Graphs

Grab Bag Graph

Place an assortment of leaves into a grab bag. (Use the leaves from the Leaf Safari activity on page 132 or gather a collection of leaves.) Have students take turns pulling a leaf from the bag and placing it in a floor graph by color, shape, and size. When the graph is completed, discuss the results with students.

Picture Graph

Using the picture cards from the game Leaf Litter, have students work cooperatively to graph the picture cards according to the type of leaf—*compound, simple,* or *needle*. Students could use a pocket chart or floor graph to graph the cards or just arrange them on a table or on the floor. When the graph is completed, discuss the results with students.

Answer Key—page 172

Independent Graph

Make a copy for each student of the Leaf Litter Graphing Sheet and Graphing Picture Cards on pages 149 and 150. Have students cut apart the picture cards, then glue the picture cards on the graphing sheet to show the types of leaves—compound, simple, or needle. This exercise can be used as an assessment tool.

Answer Key—page 172

Leaf
Litter

Leaf
Litter

Leaf
Litter

Leaf
Litter

10			
9			
8			
7			
6			
5			
4			
3			
2			
1			
	Simple	Compound	Needle

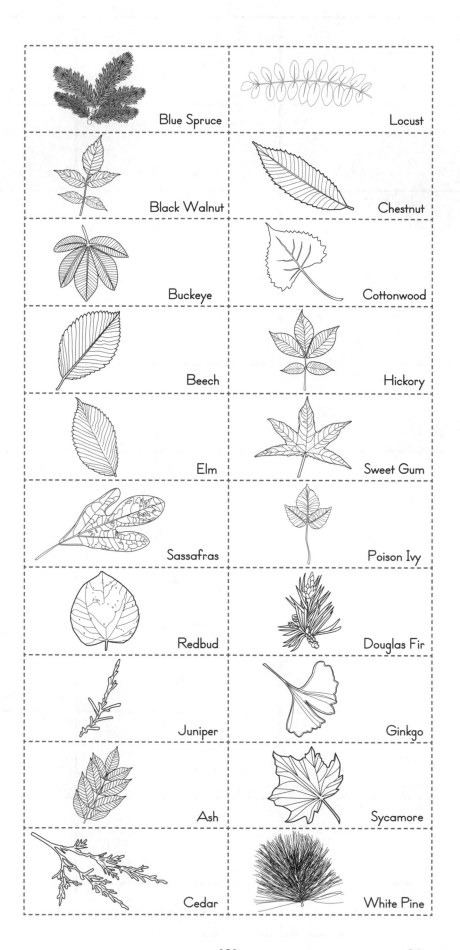

Blue Spruce

Locust

Black Walnut

Chestnut

Buckeye

Cottonwood

Beech

Hickory

Elm

Sweet Gum

Sassafras

Poison Ivy

Redbud

Douglas Fir

Juniper

Ginkgo

Ash

Sycamore

Cedar

White Pine

Zany Zoo

Life Science—The Characteristics of Organisms

- Organisms have basic needs. Animals need air, water, and food.

Life Science—Life Cycles of Organisms

- Many characteristics of an organism are inherited from the parents.

Life Science—Organisms and Their Environments

- An organism's patterns of behavior are related to the nature of that organism's environment.

 **Tidbits for Teachers**

Animal Movements

- Animals move to find food, shelter, a mate, and to escape danger. Animal movements are an adaptation to the animal's environment.

Fly

- Animals that move through the air (fly) need wings. Strong chest muscles are necessary to flap wings.
- Flying animals are lightweight. Birds have fewer bones than most animals. The bones they have are hard but thin. Some birds have bones weighing less than their feathers!
- Flying takes lots of energy so flying animals must eat often.
- Birds, bats, and flies have two wings. Butterflies, bees, and moths have four wings.
- Flying allows some animals to migrate great distances.
- Birds fly higher and faster than any other animal. Flying is useful to escape danger on the ground.
- Some birds can't fly (penguins, ostriches). Bats are the only mammals that fly. Some squirrels, lizards, and frogs have flaps of skin that they spread out and give the appearance of flying by gliding through the air.

Hop

- Animals that hop have big, strong hind legs and large feet.
- Long tails sometimes help provide balance for animals that hop.
- Hopping is a very efficient movement. Hopping marsupials like kangaroos and wallabies can increase their speed without expending additional energy.

Swim

- Water animals have fins, webbed feet, and/or flippers.
- Some animals, like frogs, have webbed feet for swimming. Webbed feet provide power and speed. Tortoises and penguins have flippers to push through the water.
- Many swimming animals have the ability to breathe under water—fish, sharks, some crabs. Some swimming animals must come to the surface to breathe—whales, turtles, penguins, seals.

Walk

- Land animals have four limbs. Some use all four limbs to walk and others use only two limbs to move.
- The greater the foot area that touches the ground when an animal walks, the slower it moves.
- Broad feet spread an animal's weight out over larger areas to help it stay on top of snow and sand.
- Surface tension helps some animals walk on water.
- Cheetahs are the fastest land animals.

Energizing Exploration: Kinesthetic Connection

To introduce the topic of animal movements, give your students the opportunity to demonstrate what they already know through their own movements! Choose an animal that hops, one that walks, one that swims, and one that flies (examples: bunny, cheetah, fish, and bird). Ask the students to spread out around the room. Name each animal aloud and allow the students to "become" the animal. Record on a poster or chart all the characteristics that the students acted out. When your class is finished acting like and discussing each animal, circle the word for each animal that describes how that animal moves. Ask the students what all the circled words have in common. Discuss as a class the different ways that animals move. Brainstorm lists of other animals that hop, walk, swim, and fly.

Energizing Exploration: Music Movements

Tell students that they are going to hop, walk, swim, or fly to music. Play a variety of music, such as classical, rap, jazz, hip hop or country, and encourage students to move to the music.

Energizing Exploration: Animal Antics

There are so many games you can play to reinforce all the different ways that animals move!

- Play animal movement charades.

- Play Duck, Duck, Goose, substituting the names of different animals for the "goose." For example, if the person who is "it" says "rabbit," then the two students have to hop around the circle back to the starting point.

- Set up an obstacle course of cones with animal pictures on the cones. When the students get to a cone, they move like the animal pictured.

- Divide the class into two teams on opposite sides of the playground or gym. Show one team an animal picture. That team then does the animal movement toward the other team. The other team must guess what animal they are imitating before they reach them.

- Divide the class into small groups and let each group create a simple dance that contains the animal movements hop, walk, swim, and fly. Let each group perform their dance and teach it to the class.

- Use the animal movements hop, walk, swim, and fly throughout the school day to travel to various activities. For example, hop like a bunny to lunch or walk slowly like a turtle to recess.

Zany Zoo

Life Science—Organisms and Their Environments

Objective: To identify animal movements as walk, swim, fly, and hop.

Preparation

1. Remove and assemble the Zany Zoo game board (pages 156, 157, 160, and 161). Mount the game board on poster board or oak tag and attach the answer key to the back (page 172). Laminate the game board.

2. Laminate and cut out the Zany Zoo picture cards (pages 163, 165, and 167).

3. Cut out and laminate the Zany Zoo Directions card (below).

4. Store the Zany Zoo picture cards in a resealable storage bag. Label the bag with the game name label (page 175).

   Note: It is important to review each set of picture cards with students before playing a game. Some pictures could be interpreted in more than one way.

Zany Zoo Directions

Materials

- Zany Zoo game board
- Zany Zoo picture cards

  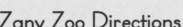 

How to Play the Game

2–4 players

1. Shuffle the Zany Zoo picture cards and place them facedown beside the game board.

2. Take turns drawing a picture card. For each card, decide if the animal moves by walking, swimming, flying, or hopping. Place the card in the correct box.

3. Continue taking turns until all the cards have been placed on the board.

4. Remove each stack of cards separately and check them against the answer key.

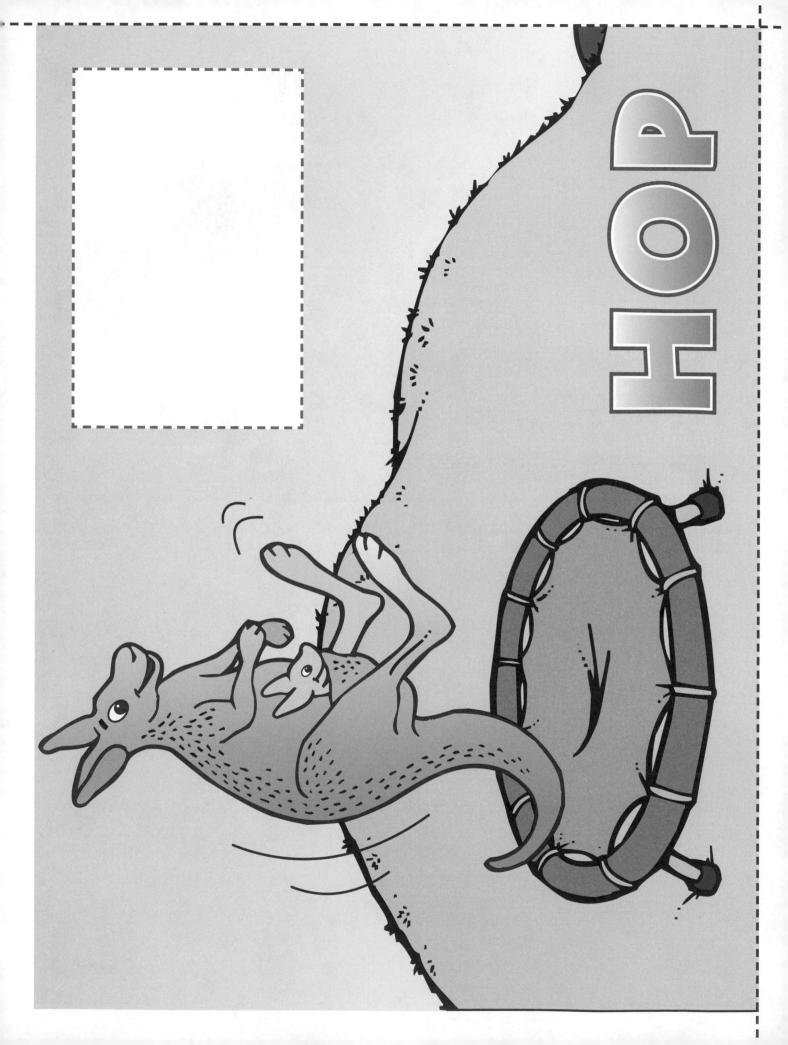

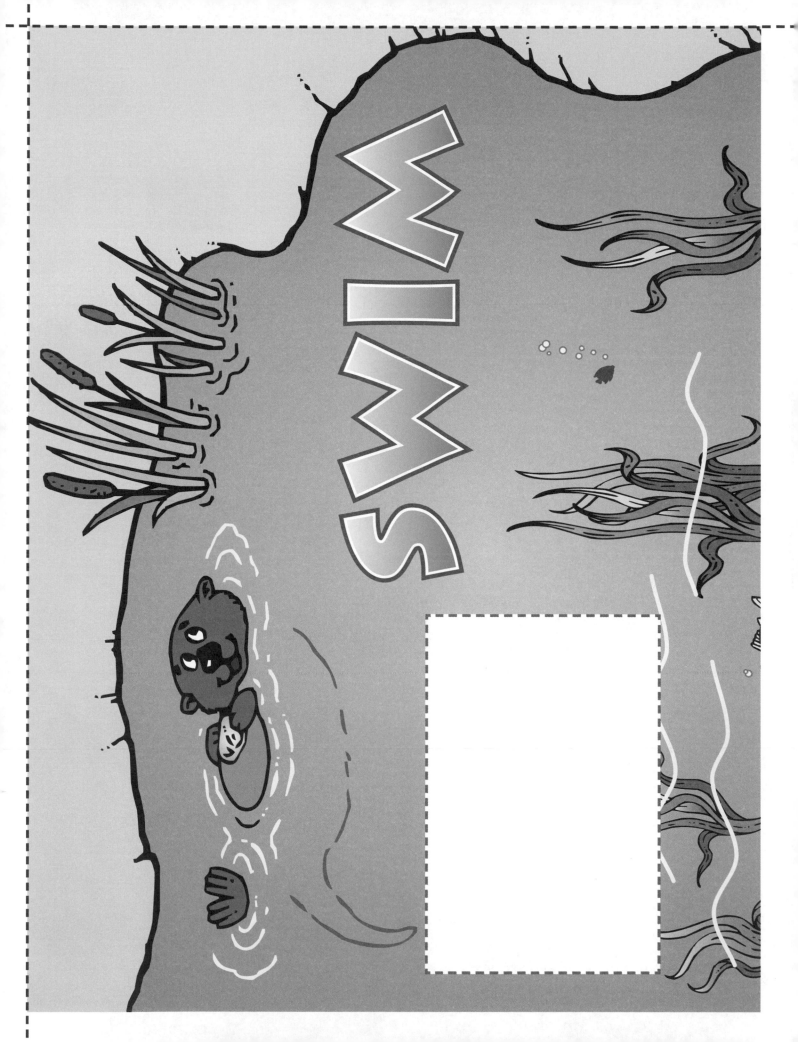

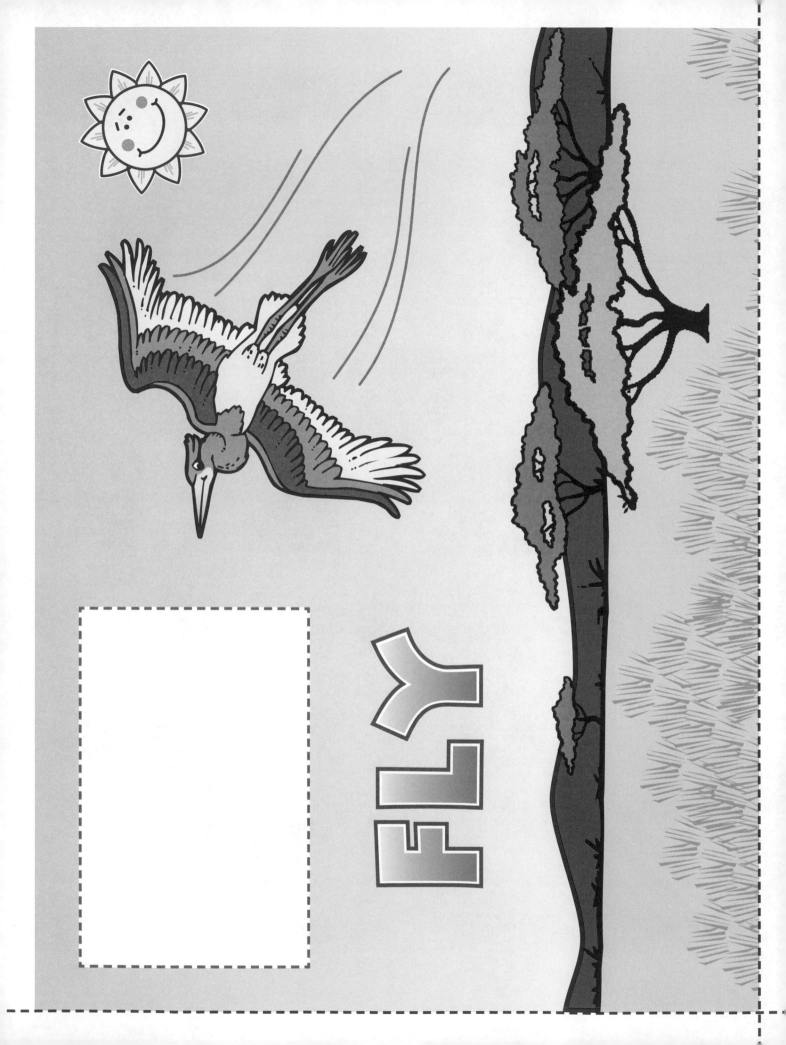

FLY

WALK

Zany
Zoo

Zany
Zoo

Zany
Zoo

Zany
Zoo

Zany
Zoo

Zany
Zoo

Zany
Zoo

Zany
Zoo

Zany
Zoo

Zany
Zoo

Zany
Zoo

Zany
Zoo

Zany
Zoo

Zany
Zoo

Zany
Zoo

Zany
Zoo

Great Graphs

Animal Cracker Sort

Provide each student with a small cup of animal crackers. Have students sort and classify their animal crackers as the teacher directs—big/small, wild/tame, movements, zoo, farm, etc. Students will enjoy eating their animal crackers when they are finished!

Picture Graph

Using the picture cards from the game Zany Zoo, have students work cooperatively to graph the picture cards according to the type of animal movement—walk, fly, swim, hop. Students could use a pocket chart or a floor graph to graph the cards or just arrange them on a table or on the floor.

When the graph is completed, discuss the results with students.

Answer Key—page 172

Independent Graph

Make a copy for each student of the Zany Zoo Graphing Sheet and Graphing Picture Cards on page 169 and 170. Have students cut apart the picture cards, then glue the picture cards on the graphing sheet to show the animal movements—walk, fly, swim, hop. This exercise can be used as an assessment tool.

Answer Key—page 172

Zany
Zoo

Zany
Zoo

Zany
Zoo

Zany
Zoo

7				
6				
5				
4				
3				
2				
1				
	Hop	Swim	Fly	Walk

Answer Key

Note: Not all cards are used on graphing pages.

Push and Pull	Sink or Float	Mighty Materials	Winter Ways
Push	**Sink**	**Wood**	**Hibernate**
elevator buttons	marbles	pencil	Turtle
stroller	rock	picnic table	Frog
lawn mower	key	rocking chair	Brown Bat
scooter	grapes	fence	Snake
doorbell	paper clip	desk	Chipmunk
grocery cart	coins	door	Ladybird Beetle
bulldozer	rubber band	blocks	Groundhog
bulldozer	buttons		
tractor	soap	**Metal**	**Migrate**
	clothespin	silverware	Dragonfly
Pull		keys	Canadian Goose
rope	**Float**	chain	Monarch Butterfly
zipper	toothbrush	hand saw	Robin
weed	sponge	whistle	Gray Whale
tow truck	paper	hanger	
water skier	candle	cooking pot	**Adapt**
rabbit in a hat	craft stick	tuba	Snowshoe Rabbit
bow and arrow	apple		Weasel
dog sled	cork	**Paper**	Fox
carrot	leaf	brown bag	Deer
carrot	pencil	wrapping paper	Snowy Owl
loose tooth	twig	road map	Crow
		notepad	Wolf
		envelope with letter	Turkey

Answer Keys (CONT.)

Note: Not all cards are used on graphing pages

Tempting Temperatures	Night and Day	Playground Pleasures	Leaf Litter	Zany Zoo
Hot	**Night**	**Living**	**Simple**	**Hop**
swimsuit	flashlight	girl	Sweet Gum	grasshopper
flip flops	pillow	boy	Cottonwood	frog
sunglasses	pajamas	dog	Redbud	rabbit
sunscreen	candle	cat	Ginkgo	kangaroo
lemonade	lamp	tree	Chestnut	toad
swimming	night light	flower	Elm	
sprinkler		butterfly	Sassafras	**Walk**
sun	**Day**	squirrel	Sycamore	rhino
camel	tricycle	crow	Beech	tiger
cactus	slide	bird		cow
	lunchbox	grass	**Compound**	moose
Cold	box of cereal		Hickory	camel
coat	sunglasses	**Non-living**	Ash	
mittens	sunscreen	rock	Black Walnut	**Swim**
earmuff	backpack	sand	Buckeye	whale
snow boots	lawn mover	bench	Poison ivy	shark
hot chocolate	alarm clock	fountain	Locust	seal
snowman	**Both Night and Day**	slide		octopus
igloo	television	ball	**Needle**	
shoveling snow	toothbrush	bucket	Blue Spruce	**Fly**
penguin	book	shovel	Juniper	dragonfly
snowflakes	rubber duck	bicycle	Cedar	butterfly
	fork		Douglas Fir	robin
			White Pine	eagle
				bumble bee
				parrot

Dear Parents,

In class we used this game to reinforce a particular science concept.

It was so much fun that we decided to send it home so your child could show off his or her science knowledge.

Please allow your child to teach you how to play. Enjoy watching your child's interest in science grow!

Return this game by _____ _____ so that another child can enjoy an evening of family science fun!

Wishing you lots of family fun!

_____

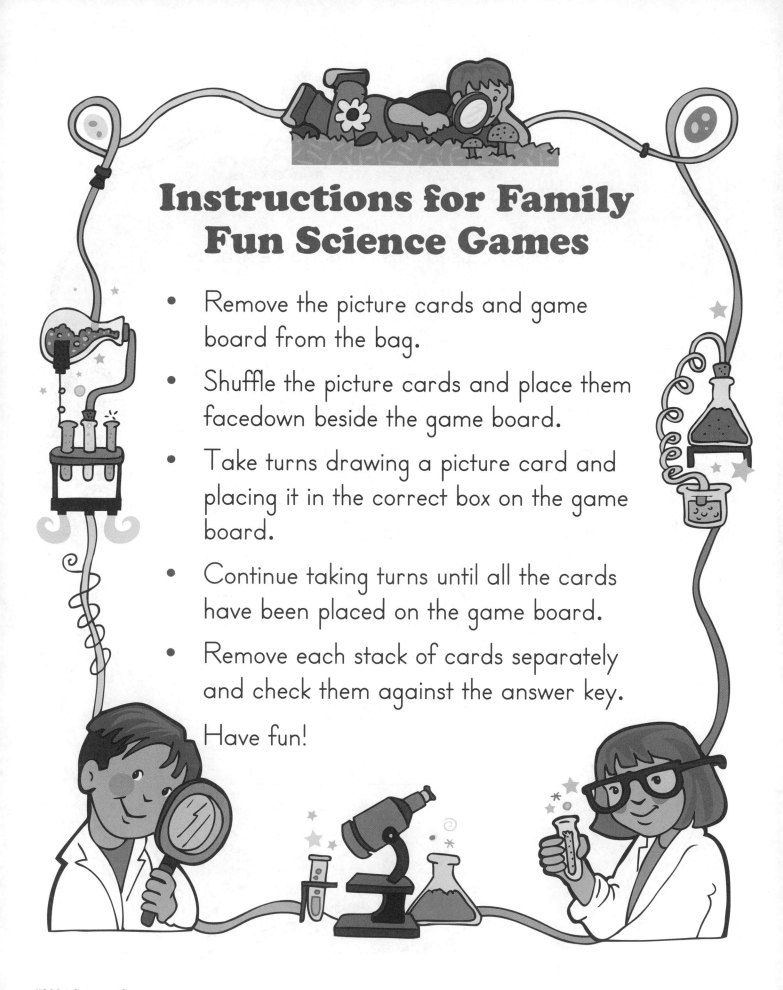

Instructions for Family Fun Science Games

- Remove the picture cards and game board from the bag.

- Shuffle the picture cards and place them facedown beside the game board.

- Take turns drawing a picture card and placing it in the correct box on the game board.

- Continue taking turns until all the cards have been placed on the game board.

- Remove each stack of cards separately and check them against the answer key.

Have fun!

Game Labels

Push and Pull

Sink or Float

Mighty Materials

Winter Ways

Tempting Temperatures

Night and Day

Playground Pleasures

Leaf Litter

Zany Zoo